MUSINGS

FROM

God's Lieutenant

Bert Hudnall

Musings from God's Lieutenant

ISBN: 1-890306-29-0

Library of Congress Control Number: 2001088444

Warwick House Publishing
720 Court Street
Lynchburg, Virginia

Table of Contents

Introduction

One day when I was fifteen years old, my dad said to me, "Son, I'm not blaming you for being fifteen; that's not something you can help. But what you *can* help is how you sound like you know everything there is to know. I can assure you that there is more learning ahead of you, and I earnestly hope that as you learn more, you'll talk about it less."

Well, at least I remembered what he said, and I am conscious about sounding like a know-it-all some of the time, but apparently not enough. Some forty-five years later, I am still in need of an occasional reminder to tone it down. Not long ago, when I was pontificating on something, my non-judgmental wife said in a gentle way, "It must be a terrible burden to be God's lieutenant."

The message was poignant for obvious reasons, but little did she know that she had planted the seed for a title for these musings which have been accumulated over a period of a few years in response to friends who have encouraged me to put my stories into print.

So what follows here is my rendition of the *Chicken Soup* books… things that can be read quickly and then put down until another five minutes becomes available. A cousin calls this "potty reading."

I suspect the Pulitzer Prize Committee will not be calling, but I am pretty confident most people will find something to bring a chuckle, a tear, or maybe a musing of their own.

Dedication

My life has been the inspiration for much of what's here, and so in a real sense this is dedicated to everyone I've ever known. Family and friends have made life good for me, and so, named or not within these *Musings*, this is for them... with boundless thanks for giving me a charmed life that has enabled me to see the world around me as my best resource for writing.

There are, however, some random folks I simply need to name as special influences:

Our beloved MOLLIE WINFREE of Lynchburg, Virginia, who was instrumental in introducing Martha Jane and me—in itself enough to merit not only a dedicatory comment but also immeasurable gratitude. But for the last thirty years she has been a relentless source of joy and wisdom. Since starting *Musings*, I have tried several times to write one on Mollie, but I can't. She simply defies a portrayal that does justice to her beautiful, selfless self or to the depth of love we feel for her. Forgive me, Moll Doll, for being unable to capture the "real you" in words, but do know that the real you has been our souls' sustenance.

Our friend, SUSAN TARKINGTON, also of Lynchburg, who has often encouraged this effort and who very recently did so in a compelling way. When my wife was debating a job change that would substantially reduce her income, Susan said, "Well, if Bert would only write, you'd make up the difference in no time." That wasn't a nudge, it was a slap on the back that got me going. Here's to Susan and what I pray is her very wise counsel!

My professional colleague and friend, ANN POWELL, a college counselor in Suffolk, Virginia. At a counselors' meeting not long ago, I made an announcement about the death of a former counseling associate. When I returned to the lunch table, a bit damp-eyed and drained, Ann leaned over and said, "Bert, you should write!" The timing there, too, was perfect. Thanks, Ann.

ELSA McDOWELL, a regular columnist in our Charleston paper who writes about people and things like those I write about and whose opinion I sought as added assurance that time spent on such a project wouldn't be wasted. Her lovely response was more generous than I expected, but the key line was, "You *must* write."

My aunt, ELIZABETH REVERCOMB, in Charleston, West Virginia, nearly ninety and the most avid reader I know. It was she above others who, fifteen years ago or so when I wrote a dinky little twenty-five recipe cookbook with "entertaining narrative," gave me the greatest boost by purchasing copies for her friends. (Footnote: a few of those books are still around for anyone who may want them for the pittance of $4.00.)

Our cousins, NANCY and JIM REVERCOMB, in Roanoke, Virginia, the essence of encouragers in everything, who have always taken time to show interest in other people's interests. Nancy and Jim have given me confidence I suspect they have no idea about.

MELISSA WHITE, the office manager for the Junior League of Charleston, South Carolina, and my invaluable assistant/ typist/ coordinator for this little book. It would have been enough for her to do so ably what I would have taken hours and hours to do, but she added to her talents a wonderful graciousness when she said, "I love reading these." The perfect lagniappe!

And speaking of lagniappes, that's exactly what I hope *Musings* will be for you.

She Told Him So

"Macho" and "Wimp" weren't words we knew growing up. If they had been around then, Carlyle Rose would have fancied himself as macho, when in fact he was nothing more than a bully. And I guess I would have been a wimp, at least when it came to Carlyle. He terrorized me! The mere mention of his name made me gulp twice in rapid succession, and actually seeing him scared all sorts of things out of me. Carlyle never really beat me up, but he would jab me and shove me. The really terrifying thing, though, was the threats he would mutter in a sinister way while squinting his already slitty eyes. I presumed that one day I would be pulverized by Carlyle, and the pall that that likelihood cast over me was more consuming than the World War going on at the time. Rumor had it that Carlyle had hit his mother with a poker and thrown her into a closet. With that as a gauge for what may lie in store for me, I trembled even when I thought I might spy Carlyle at a distance.

When my mother would ask me to go to the grocery store, a route that took me right past Carlyle's house, I prayed Carlyle would be doing something (maybe hitting his mother again) that would keep him from seeing me pass by. My mother knew of my fear, but because Carlyle had never actually hurt me, she didn't seem to be as sympathetic as I would have liked. Either she thought it wasn't a serious concern, or she privately hoped the whole thing would toughen me up. Whatever, I was surprised, but also horrified, when Mom said to me one day, "I ran into Carlyle Rose today and told him that he'd be well advised to leave you alone. I told him you were a strong boy, and if he ever provoked you enough you would probably haul off and hit him so hard he'd regret it for the rest of his life." Well, she might as well have escorted me personally to the guillotine. As far as I could tell, my days were numbered. Me hit Carlyle??!! There was a greater chance of the Leaning Tower of Pisa straightening up! And so for days I quaked, lost sleep, and nervously waited for my own personal doomsday.

Sometime after that on a Saturday, some friends and I went to a movie, and when it was over I decided to take a short cut home, using a narrow passageway between two buildings. Evidently, Carlyle had spotted me, and he lay in wait for me at the end of that little walk. As I emerged into the open area at the end, Carlyle jumped at me. The shock was so great that I threw out my arms with tremendous force, and one of them landed squarely on Carlyle's nose, breaking it and causing the blood to flow. He was stunned. Realizing that I had hurt him much more than he had ever hurt me, I lit out for home screaming bloody murder and convinced that each breath was my last. To my astonishment, I finally noticed that Carlyle was not chasing me. I wasn't sure why, but I was very glad.

The next time I saw Carlyle, he turned and walked away before I could. That was a very good sign. And when I told my mother, her nonchalant reply was, "I warned him."

Early Greek writers and artists called on the Muses for inspiration before beginning to work.
World Book Encyclopedia

(I wish I'd known!)

A Tale of Two Friends

Frank and Tom: two friends with two very different backgrounds and from two totally different parts of my past. They not only never met, they would never have known of each other. Frank was a Methodist minister's son who moved to my hometown when we were fifteen. We became fast friends overnight, being silly and laughing at every nonsensical thing we came across. Typical of many PK's (preacher's kids), Frank was irreverent—hilariously so. He could turn the Sunday service or a mealtime grace into a sideshow, and I would literally get hiccups from laughing so hard at him. His father was fairly humorless, which made the irreverence all the funnier. His mother was more tolerant, but nonetheless proper—so that once when she sat in a leather chair that made a sound like a fart, she was quick to say, "That was the chair." Frank said, "No way." I convulsed.

He called me "Tranny," and whenever I picked up a phone and heard "Tranny, let's..." I knew I was headed for an adventure. We went to different colleges, but stayed in touch. One summer when I was in graduate school, I got a call saying Frank was engaged to a woman named Annie who also happened to be at the same summer school as I. Annie and I became close friends, so that when I ushered in their wedding several months later I truly understood that union. Later, I became their son's godfather and visited in their home often. Laughter abounded.

A few years later, I took the stroll down the aisle myself. Frank was an usher, of course. He and Annie gave a grand party. Although we would live in different towns, there was every reason to believe we'd all be the typical "best couple friends." Our wedding was on December 2, 1972. On January 4, I opened a letter from Frank, fully expecting some zany comments about the wedding, along with a catch-up on their holiday. To the contrary, I read in stunned silence that he had left Annie and Jimmy, feeling unable and unwilling to continue with the marriage. He said more which doesn't bear repeating, but it largely was a self-flagellation laced with a "This is best for everyone" theme. A quick call to Annie found her still disbelieving and unsure of how it would all sift out. She was also unaware of his whereabouts. That was 1973. Occasional conversations with Annie and with Frank's sister revealed conjecture of everything from his death to taking on a new identity in a foreign country. The unknown was hard on everyone, including me. During that time, his father died (his mother had died earlier), and even that didn't result in new information about his whereabouts. Frank was gone, sadly.

Tom was from Toledo. He was on my hall during our freshman year at W&L. He was on the quiet side, but consistently positive. His dad had owned a meat packing business, and the family was well off, though Tom never flaunted that. He was probably the best-looking fellow I knew, but he didn't flaunt that, either. He was, at heart, shy and unassuming. One-on-one conversations late into the night revealed a person more unlike me than not, but one with whom I felt a bonding that went deep.

Tom was brighter than I, but not a student. He let his grades drop, and by the end of the sophomore year he was ineligible to return. Picking up on his military prep school background, he elected to join the Marines. Although I'm the letter writer, Tom initiated a correspondence that we maintained throughout his military service. I detected some loneliness and tried to offset it with things that would let him focus on better things ahead "soon." I laced my letters with as many grumblings about school, weather and misfortunes as possible so as not to give him anything to envy. Amid his pinings for home, Tom wrote of interesting adventures, intriguing European women, and an experience that sounded really fascinating. In fact, *I* did the envying.

He came home after I had graduated, and very different career paths and personal circumstances took their toll on our contact. It was ten years later when I was planning a trip to Oklahoma City that I remembered something about Tom's being in that area. A phone call to information confirmed my memory and another to Tom resulted in an invitation to dinner, where I met his wife and two baby daughters. The reconnection "took," and occasional notes and Christmas cards kept us abreast of key things in our respective lives, including his later divorce and a move to New Mexico where he was doing some *avant garde* theatre work, largely directing plays.

Another fifteen years passed, and a trip to Albuquerque for me found time for Tom and me to meet in my hotel lobby where we had four or five (or six) drinks each and discovered that our freshman year bonding was valid and was the foundation for a meaningful adult friendship. We searched souls together and felt a soul-brother kinship. Each one's family was important to the other. Although we thought very independently, we conversed with an uncanny depth of feeling and mutual respect. That was a singular evening in my life.

Its only edge was a persistent cough Tom had. It annoyed him and concerned me. It seemed more than a cold, but I wasn't inclined to add to his discomfort by showing alarm.

Tom never mentioned his health in subsequent communications, but in the spring of 1993 he called from San Diego to say he was in a hospital awaiting a lung transplant. He had been diagnosed with a genetic affliction which could only be reversed by a transplant. The surgery was risky and the availability of a lung was scant. His coughing was so pervasive I could hardly understand him. I detected no fear and a real hopefulness, and all the strength of character that I then realized had been his summary attraction was capsulized in that one brief conversation. A very simple "Thanks for sticking with me over the years" gave me a new determination to be loyal, but it said more about him than about me. In great adversity, he was thinking outward.

Three weeks later, Tom's brother called. "Bert, my brother Tom died today. He valued your friendship very much." "Thanks," I said, "I knew that. He had the grace to tell me so himself."

As I hung up, I shed some tears unashamedly. I felt a void immediately and mused about how one ever fills such a gap.

The phone rang again. I almost didn't answer it but consciously decided it would be good therapy to get my mind off my grief.

After my "hello," there was a short silence, and then I heard, "Tranny, this is Frank. We've got twenty years to catch up on."

I still shake my head over this thirty-minute segment in my life when I lost one friend and found another I thought was lost. I don't call it a compensation, but I do call it a blessing. And I want to call it something else—but what?

"What I mean by the Muse is that unimpeded clearness of the intuitive power...Should these faculties have free play, I believe they will open new, deeper, and purer sources of joyous inspiration than have yet refreshed the earth."
Margaret Fuller
(1810-1850)

Memorable Moments in Education

Interviewing prospective college students was almost always a good—even delightful—experience. They were often witty, confident, well-informed young people who broadened my horizons considerably. When a student was a real zinger, I often found myself going the extra mile to make her want to come to our college, and conversely, I worked hard at not letting a weak interview cloud my objectivity about the student's overall merits. That was *very* difficult one particular time.

The young woman came to our office after sending in school records that showed an A average and SAT's of 1440 in her junior year. Short of learning she was a serial killer, we were very sure she would be admitted. What we didn't know is that the term "painfully shy" was coined with her in mind. She didn't have a limp handshake; she only had a limp hand! From my smiling, "Hi, Candace, we're glad you are here" to my hasty wind-up twenty minutes later, she could do nothing more than smile with a quivering bottom lip. I kept wanting to look at myself in the mirror to see if I really had been transformed into an ogre. I knew that for both our sakes I needed to terminate this torture session, but my perverse side kicked in. So I said to her, "Candace, I could talk forever about this college and may never hit on things that matter to you, so before you have a tour, please ask me just one question about our college." Gulping and sweating, she timidly squeaked out her question: "How many coke machines do you have on campus?"

At a boarding school where I was head, we had a January Term during which students in good standing pursued approved projects in their home towns while others returned to campus from the Christmas break to be tutored in areas where they needed help.

Gloria was a girl who fell into the latter category in several subjects. She was also a girl who had proven her unreliability over and over again so that when she came tearfully to me before the Christmas break to plead being allowed to stay at home in January because "my mother is dying," I didn't know whether to believe her or not. She described a brave single parent whose days were numbered and who desperately needed Gloria's TLC just as Gloria needed to be with her. "I could never concentrate on tutoring, knowing my mother is dying—and please don't talk to Mom about this because she would insist I come back to school, but I just can't."

After agonizing over this situation for a while, I deferred to Gloria's wishes—only because I really wasn't ready to accept the guilt if, in fact, Gloria was telling the truth for a change. But as I gave her my decision, I came within an inch of saying, "If your mother doesn't die, you'll be sorry!"

Gloria returned in February with the wonderful news that her mother's illness had gone into remission.

As the admissions director at a school where I also taught English, I often needed to use evening and weekend time to catch up on backlogged correspondence. Such was the case one Sunday afternoon when I dictated dozens of letters to be transcribed the next day.

Then I strolled over to the dining hall for supper where the headmaster asked me to say the blessing. I took the microphone and asked everyone to bow heads, whereupon I began a rambling prayer that asked for God's blessings on missionaries, our maintenance staff, and almost every aggrieved person imaginable. Realizing that my weary brain needed to bring this thing to a close, but forgetting that I was holding a microphone, not a Dictaphone, I said, "If there is anything else we can be doing for you at this time, please let me hear from you. Sincerely yours...."

One of my favorite college counselor counterparts maintains that ninety percent of all calls from anxious parents emanate from grocery store or cocktail party chatter and that most of the issues being called about die quickly on the vine if left alone. At the beginning of each year, she sends the parents of seniors a questionnaire, ostensibly to "update my information," but her real reason is to ask for those times in the parents' schedules when they have standing appointments—bridge games, exercise times, volunteer obligations, etc. Then, when the parents call and leave a message to be called back for an urgent concern, my friend consults her files and returns the call when she knows the parents won't be there, leaving her own message that she was sorry to miss them. Few ever call back.

"The mother of the Muses
was Mnemosyne, meaning *memory.*
Since poetry before the days of writing had to
be memorized, it is not surprising that the
Muses were the *daughters of memory.*"
Words from the Myths
Issac Asimov

Airports

I love airports, not only because of their people-watching appeal and how they represent the quickest way to get from here to there (usually!), but also because of the life lessons I invariably learn from being in an airport or an airplane.

I've seen reunions that touched me so deeply I cried as much as those finding solace in each other's arms. I've overheard those waiting and pacing discuss their arriving loved one—a son just diagnosed with AIDS—and how they must balance their welcome so as not to let their broken hearts add to his grief, only to see all those good intentions dissolve in a flood of tears and hugs so fervent I wondered if they would ever let go.

I've seen waiting areas filled with balloons to add a gala aura to the homecoming of military men and women, and I watched as banners hailed the arrival of a jailed activist returning to freedom in her hometown. While I probably wouldn't have agreed with what she had done, I couldn't help applauding the unabashed loyalty displayed by her family and friends.

One of the more poignant welcomes I ever saw was for a young boy, maybe eighteen, who had sat beside me on the plane. He had green hair, rings in his nostril and eyebrow, and eyes that bespoke abuse and unhappiness. Shamefully, I wasn't inclined to strike up a conversation, nor was he. But as we were about to land, I asked if he were from Charleston. His terse "Yeah" let me know I needn't probe more. Then as the plane touched down, he let out an audible sigh, "Jesus!" And then he blurted out, "This is bad, man. I'm seeing my parents for the first time since I ran away two years ago." I wanted to say, It'll be OK, but I suspected it really wouldn't be.

We deplaned together, I in front of him. I saw the parents before he did—perfectly groomed, professional people with a well-scrubbed daughter who had to be the head cheerleader somewhere. I almost couldn't watch, but I'm so glad I did. What I saw was unqualified love abound as the four of them locked arms and buried their heads so close they might have had trouble breathing.

Airport reunions can also be amusing. Once I saw a boy meet a girl in a moment that cried out "AWKWARD!" The dialogue went something like this:

He: "What's up?"

She: "How're you doin'?"

He: "What's new?"

She: "How ya' been?"

He: "What's happenin'?"

She: "How's it goin'?"

They faded out of earshot before I could learn if they ever stopped asking questions and uttered a declarative statement.

They all are indelible impressions, but the one I choke up over the most was seeing the strapping thirty-year-old man rush to the woman being wheeled off the plane, lift her powerfully but gently from the wheelchair with a "Hi, beautiful girl," and then say to the attendant, "Thanks for looking after my mom; I'll take her from here." He strode down the concourse carrying her like a cherished prize. I fully expected to see him raise her high and yell, "I won!"

I prefer not to have planes delayed, but when that happens I usually see or hear something that fascinates, amuses, or touches me. I'm a better person for what many strangers have unwittingly done to inspire me.

On Fleeing Hurricanes

As a mountaineer by birth, I find the hurricane season of my new area of residence to be fascinating—and very unsettling. Don't get me wrong. It isn't the hurricane threats that unsettle me, it's the fear that I'll reveal myself as being totally inept in talking the language and "doing the right thing" as people brace for Hurricane Xavier or his sister Jezebel. Fortunately, we have kind neighbors who know we are green in hurricane ways, and they remind us that, for example, lawn chairs can be deadly missiles in a fierce storm. Heeding such advice, we have found ourselves virtually denuding our yard of anything that isn't planted by God. Once done and preening over our savvy handling of that task, we then talk to someone who says, "Oh, we never do that. We prefer to spend our time securing valuable art work and crystal." That, of course, sends us into frantic action to do that very thing (with the word "valuable" as a key, it doesn't take us long). Once accomplished, we manage to mention our activity to another person who says, "We prefer to spend our time collecting the really irreplaceable things, such as photographs." Another good idea, and so off we go to pull together one-of-a-kind pictures, the process for which gets bogged down as we find whole drawers of pictures we haven't thought about for twenty-five years and which require deliberate sorting-through to the point of foolishness in view of Xavier breathing down our necks. In addition to learning just what matters to each of several people as they do their hurricane preparations, we are also aware that hurricanes make for excellent telephone gossip which, the truth be known, probably takes more time than everything else. The really interesting revelation is that we now do all the things that each advisor seemed to have time for only one of.

When Hurricane Floyd moved our way with his biggest-ever reputation, we detected added concern from some friends. One of them, who had once said that he slept through Hugo in 1989, seemed slightly less brave this time. When I asked if he intended to stay again, he replied, "I'm no fool." Nothing more needs to be said here on that subject. Harking back to all the advice we had been given before, we quickly took care of the lawn missiles and the household valuables. Given Floyd's impressive credentials, we also moved every movable piece of furniture to the second floor to save things from potential water damage (never mind that we expected to find no roof upon returning). Then we gathered portable valuables such as photographs, the silver service, and some jewelry. My wife was to take the dog in her car, and I had Tim, the cat, who hates cars so much that he has diarrhea and throws up amid a constant howling. Knowing that our destination point was three and a half hours away and my wife had driven Tim to Charleston (eight hours) when we moved, I accepted this as my obligation. Just as we were about to leave, she said to me, "Since we don't know when we'll be back, don't you think you ought to take a suit so that you can make some business calls if they should crop up?" Thinking that was an inspired thought, I dashed back upstairs, quickly chose a suit, and then spent a full five minutes going through my ties to find a good match! Realizing the lunacy of sorting through ties on the brink of being blown away by a catastrophic storm, I pulled all of them off the rack—all seventy-seven of them—and stashed them into a canvas bag. Then we were off!

Four hours later, we had gotten as far as the Charleston airport, normally twenty minutes away. Traffic was alternately at a standstill or moving a few inches per half hour. We were able to remain in tandem since there was never enough space between us for anyone to squeeze in. Several times when we were stopped, one of us would visit with the other. At one point, Martha Jane asked, "What are you thinking about while we are stuck like this?" I could honestly say that I hadn't thought about anything much. Watching other people, some of whom had become very familiar under the circumstances, had been somewhat fun, and listening to our governor praise us for our cooperation and say that he was taking the opening of other interstate lanes under advisement had been somewhat off-putting but a timetaker. And then the age-old truism that misery loves company kept coming to mind. Lord knows, there was a lot of misery and everyone had a lot of company.

The Floyd tales will doubtless abound for years. And even if they take on new dimensions over time, as stories are wont to do, it is safe to say that everyone will believe every exaggeration because in truth it *could* have happened.

OH, there *is* one thing I thought about while idling during one twenty-minute period: I may have been silly to have labored over a tie choice, but in the final analysis, my seventy-seven ties were probably more valuable than the silver and jewelry put together! With that revelation, I now have my own bit of advice to offer novice hurricane evacuees, or refugees, as we were also referred to: SAVE YOUR TIES!

There were Nine Muses. Three were:
Calliope — epic poetry
Erato — love poetry
Euterpe — lyric poetry

Tammy Lou Is About to Be a Grandmother

She is approaching that time when she will be expected to knit booties, do some quilting, and put up pickles, just like grandmothers are supposed to do. Does it strike anyone else that grandmotherly types aren't supposed to be named Tammy Lou?

Grandmothers are Marthas, Louisas, Cornelias, Charlottes, Mathildas, Helens, Dorothys, Gertrudes, Elizabeths (or one of the several shortened forms like Betty, Betsy, and Bess, but not Beth, Lisa, or Lillybet). Speaking of Gertrude, I confess that every time I see an obituary for a Gertrude, I think we're one step closer to an extinct name in this country.

But not in Germany, of course, from which the only Gertrude I know in my generation came. And speaking of Germany, what's their equivalent of Tammy Lou? Surely, each country has its trendy, new names, but I can't think any place beats us.

Names are a highly personal thing, and who among us, especially me, can or should stand in judgment about something over which absolutely no one has any control? But while I never really liked my name because it comes off sounding stuffy and a little irregular, I was always glad to have it because of its namesake, my grandfather. The same is true with everyone in my family, named for someone(s) whose legacy was valued. My daughter is named Elizabeth, as was my mother, my grandmother, an aunt, and a few cousins. My wife has joked that naming a daughter Elizabeth was a condition of marriage. My wife is Martha Jane, after both grandmothers and epitomizing the double-name, Southern thing. I was in my late twenties before it was ever called to my attention that double names weren't the norm worldwide and that, in fact, they are dead giveaways for southerners. The reason I was so slow in understanding this is that among my closest friends in my small Virginia hometown were Sara Lu, Mollie Jo, Mary Carolyn, Sue

Ellen, Helen Jean, Anna Seward, Frances Neale and Sally—and she was the suspicious one since she could easily have been called Sara Nair after her well-known grandmother. True, several of these girls' families had found an out-of-the-sky middle name for their daughters, but every one of the first names was for someone "significant."

Double names can, however, be stretched in the interest of "keeping it family." My wife had a dance teacher known far and wide as Julia Mildred. To me, they don't go together, and even frequent repetition doesn't give it the ring it needs. I've known others whose sense of rhythm was a bit off, not aware that "Fay Lisa" or "Jean Mollie" don't "go."

Another name phenomenon I find fascinating is the increasing use of nicknames as real names: Nikki, Sandy, Frankie, Joanie. Such names make me come back to the grandmother thing again. Grandma Nikki?

Names are inspired by stars. In my generation, Shirley Temple was often the namesake for babies, making Shirley a frequently-heard name on school rosters in the forties. An aside: My grandfather delivered most of the babies in our town including me and including the scads of Shirley Temple namesakes. In truth, most of those babies didn't stand a prayer of ever resembling Shirley Temple, but the mothers always thought they were beautiful—as mothers should! One day, a Shirley Temple mother strolling her own Shirley Temple encountered my grandfather on a downtown street and effused, "Dr. Hudnall, you haven't seen our Shirley in awhile. Doesn't she look just like Shirley Temple?" My grandfather stifled the urge to say, You've got to be kidding! and instead said, "Now *that* is a baby." The mother beamed and strolled away. Miss America of 1950 was Yolande Betbeze. Now look back to how many forty-years-olds have that rather uncommon name. I'm not sure who inspired the Tiffany rage, but it certainly took hold and continues to be at the top of many charts.

Variant spellings of names fascinate me. The simple, nice name Amy has been given such distinctive spellings as Ami, Aimee, Ammee (phonetically not OK), and the one that really got me—Aymy. One year at the small women's school where I was admissions director, we had seven freshmen named Carrie—or Cary, Carey, Kerry, Kerri, Keri, and, of course, Kharry. These were not to be confused with Cara, Kara, Kira. Nor was Kristen to be confused with Christen, Kirsten, Kirstie, or Christa.

Maybe the thing I can in good conscience pick at is misspellings which become "real" names and don't have any basis in logic. Keep your eye out for the number of people named Sheila who spell it Shelia and still keep it two syllables. That would be like pronouncing Amelia as if it were Ameila. Another one is the pretty name Deirdre which, because of mispronunciations, has too often become Deidre. And, as we Americans are wont to do, that mispronunciation has been stretched to become Deedra.

It's a little scary to realize that many babies are named on a whim for a TV show's star, the local Tiny Miss Dumplingcake, or some circumstance. One recent mother confessed that her baby's name had come from the birth announcements in the previous week's newspaper. Born a week later, Cassaundra Gwynette might have been LaToyetta Charrisse who, as I think about it, probably did get a namesake in some form or another.

This name thing has become such a fixation for me that I note it when I come across a new baby with one of the "good old names." Last week, I met someone with three daughters. I couldn't resist asking their names and was genuinely stunned when I heard Lucy, Ruth, and Frances.

Back to Elizabeth, my daughter. When she was born, the nurse who wheeled my wife from the delivery room asked, "What are you going to name her?" When we replied proudly, "Elizabeth," the nurse in all good conscience replied with a hearty chuckle, "No, I mean seriously." Never was I more aware that differences in this world do exist and are, I guess, important. I just think that my differences are better.

The Widows' Thanksgiving

My growing up years were wonderful. I know that now in retrospect. It wasn't mainly that I didn't want for anything; it's that I had the kinds of things that give life a deeper meaning, which are also the kinds of things which, when absent, can cause despair because of the depth of the void they leave.

My mother was the youngest of seven children and the only girl. Because she was "the girl," it fell her lot to "do Thanksgiving" when her parents died. And so each Thanksgiving, her in-town brothers, their wives and families, and an occasional in-law holiday visitor assembled at our house for a repast that satisfied everyone for the rest of the weekend. The extent of the spread isn't so important, and it was fairly predictable, but it was so special. Mama didn't really like to cook, and so she always had good help; but she did like to prepare tomato aspic (invariably called Miss Elizabeth's asbestos by one of the help), and people raved about it dutifully.

As years went by, some of the brothers died. The surviving ones began to spend their holidays with their own offspring, and the Thanksgiving dinner became less an event. And then my father died. For all practical purposes, that signaled the end of anything specially planned—or so I thought.

As Thanksgiving approached that year, my mother called me and said, "It would be so easy to do away with our Thanksgiving dinner this year, but I don't want to. There are too many widows in this town who don't have holiday plans. Let's have dinner for them... but you'll have to be the bartender!" The ring in her voice and the sense that this was the right thing to do gave me an exhilaration that I hadn't expected.

Besides bartending, I also chauffeured. I ran a regular jitney service from house to house, picking up ten or eleven women who had probably been ready an hour before the appointed time. They were old family friends, and the glee they showed gave the holiday a spirit that little else could have produced.

The memory of those ladies in their wool dresses, pretty pins, and plenty of color in their cheeks is as indelible as anything in my mind. So is their bar order: "Bourbon on the rocks, with just a splash of water." Evidently I frequently overdid the splash, because round two didn't mention water.

How does this even remotely relate to having a good adolescence? I believe it is this very kind of thing that sustains us all in times of discomfort. And I believe it is almost a duty of mine to provide something akin to it for my own children, most especially because they are growing up in such a fast-paced time when it's hard to settle down and appreciate some of life's more subtle pleasures.

And yet, I think it's happening. They say that men marry women like their mothers. I've done that. In matters of spirit, my wife is like my mother. She puts all others before herself at all times, and although our family isn't as large as my mother's, we have established a tradition whereby she makes Thanksgiving every bit the memory for my children that it was for me. The scale is smaller, but the joy is the same. Among those present always is Mollie, an eighty-five-year-old friend with life and love so abundant our world is always made better by her presence.

Who knows what the complexion of Thanksgiving will be in years to come? For now, I take heart that my children have come to understand that this kind of giving is laying a foundation for happiness in future years.

Those Good Ole' College Days

My memories of college are every bit as meaningful as anyone else's—the friends and parties, the professor who gave learning a new dimension, the late hours which, in retrospect, weren't so bad, the favorite haunts which, in retrospect, really were pretty bad, and so much else. Regrettably, but probably not uniquely, my memories also include a few ignominious moments.

One occurred as I was going through fraternity rush. I was a young-looking seventeen-year-old with a crew cut and a thirteen-inch neck accentuated by an Adam's apple which accounted for most of those thirteen inches. I wasn't a party animal, but I was perfectly willing to strike the pose that would, hopefully, offset the youthful appearance. Yet, as I went from fraternity house to fraternity house, I was admittedly uncomfortable with all the beer that was thrust into my hand and even more with all that was wasted because I really couldn't keep up. At the Delta Tau Delta house, a fraternity known for attracting the top athletes, I decided not to continue the sham and simply put my beer on the mantel behind me, telling everyone who offered a "cool one" that I was fine and pointing to the beer behind me. At one point, though, as I was being grilled by about eight of the brothers, I felt I needed at least to take an obligatory sip from my beer. My elbow was already awkwardly propped on the mantel at head height in some feeble effort to look relaxed, and without looking back I raised my hand to the mantel to retrieve my beer and came down with a small trophy. The rectifying move was no less embarrassing as I knocked over a few other trophies and my beer, all amid assurances that "these things happen." Of course, I didn't get invited back, and of course, I wouldn't have gone if I had been.

My mother had instilled in me the importance of keeping up with my elderly uncles and aunts while I was at college, and as a rule I was good about it. However, as I became more involved, I also became lax about writing, and so one Sunday afternoon I must have written ten letters to family and family friends to give them an update on my activities and well-being (and to get my mother off my back). When I had finished that marathon task, I re-read an English paper I had written, wrote out the honor pledge attesting to its being my work, and went to bed. Several days later when the paper was returned, the professor's note under the grade was a bit baffling. It read, "The sentiment is nice, but I still can't justify anything higher than a C+." As I was about to ask for a clarification, I glanced at the pledge which read, "On my honor, I have received no help in writing this paper. Love, Bert."

We were not allowed to have cars as freshmen and weren't even supposed to drive, but one evening when an upperclassman backed out of taking us to a neighboring women's college for dates we had arranged, we pled to borrow his car and he relented. We asked for directions. We followed them explicitly and had no trouble at all reaching the school. But we were surprised at seeing no one at all, and so I went into the nearest building, which turned out to be the gymnasium, to find someone who could tell us what to do from here. I was just making the indelicate observation that girls' gyms don't smell any better than boys' when a security officer came by and asked if he could help. I said, "Yes, thanks. Can you tell us where we should go to pick up our dates?" Changing tones immediately, he grunted, "Whaddya' mean, fella?" Thinking he was being overly protective, I replied in a flip tone, "Dates! You know, people you go out with. Just tell us where the freshman dorm is." Relenting just a bit, he said, "I'm hoping you think you are at Mary Baldwin. This is Staunton Military Academy."

A Traitor To My Gender

None of what follows has a shred of scientific support. It is observation and experience-based. And, as with almost everything, there are many exceptions. But amid all these demurrers, I feel very strongly about this: women are the stronger sex—stronger emotionally, spiritually, "constitutionally," and sometimes even physically. I believe that much of what it is that makes them strong has to do with a high tolerance level. Purely and simply, women are more accepting. To be sure, they are much more accepting of differences than men are.

In my experience at an all men's college, the athletes preferred being with other athletes, the artistic guys found other artistic guys, the goof-offs gravitated to other goof-offs, and the serious students were most comfortable with other serious students.

In the girls' schools and women's colleges with which I've had some association, differences seemed almost to be an attraction. At a women's college, it is not unusual to see the head cheerleader type rapt in conversation with the oversized young woman who has never had a date. I once remember hearing a Phi Beta Kappa physics major (woman) say, "I maintain my sanity by enjoying the company of artists."

While one of the greatest disservices (and untruths) is the allegation that women's colleges breed lesbianism, it's certainly true that, as on virtually every college campus, there are lesbians on single-sex campuses. It's not unusual to see the exceedingly social, heterosexual, fraternity sweetheart being tolerant of, and even sociable with, the open lesbian, with no hint of feeling threatened, but would you find the male jock caught dead within twenty feet of a known gay? Not on a bet!

Women may have historically been portrayed as the whimpering weaker sex, but such a label would hold no water today. Without dredging up specific examples that could only open wounds, I can think of many instances when the woman who had lost a loved one not only held up in the face of her loss, but also provided support and strength for those around her. Men handle such things differently, but not better.

What about spiritual strengths? Who's to gauge that? Certainly not me! But I would suggest that the next time you listen to a dull sermon, stay awake by doing a quick poll of the non-couples in the pews. Women will be there in two-to-one numbers, I'll bet you. They just aren't as inclined to go fishing, play golf, or sleep in, I suppose. This really may not accurately tell about greater spirituality in women, but I believe it does at least speak to greater self-discipline. Isn't it reasonable to think women could have agendas akin to fishing and golf to keep them out of church?

To say that women are superior in physical strength probably doesn't fly. If you were to line up ten men bodybuilders and ten women bodybuilders, I suspect men would win all strength tests. There might be an exception or two like the filly who beats her stallion competitors at the races, but the odds are not good. And horses aren't people.

On the other hand, I've come home from a day at work to find whole rooms rearranged, which required moving beds, chests, chaises—all on a carpet and rugs, and the only person at home all day was my 5'3," 120-pound wife, who greeted me fresh-faced and perky, saying, "How do you like it?" Now, I could have done all that, but I wouldn't have. And that gets us back to that other kind of strength I noted—the tolerance-related things.

Speaking of tolerance as it relates to strength, I, like most human beings, love being tolerated for all my foibles and am happy to abrogate any claim to strength in that context.

Maybe I'm not a traitor after all—just smart.

Podiatrically Challenged

I have the quickest, best-coordinated hands I know of anywhere. I tossed my children into the air with every confidence that I'd catch them. I catch flies in mid-air on the first try, and I can grab dropped dishes before they hit the floor. When we moved, my wife thought nothing of pitching the china to me from the packing box for me to put into the cupboard—nothing was even chipped. The degree of reliability where my hands are concerned is quite high. My legs and feet, however, are another story altogether.

Sometimes I have the distinct feeling that at least one of them belongs to someone else and is being operated by remote control from afar. Taking a walk scares me more than juggling raw eggs. Every surface designed for walking has its special pitfalls for me. Newly waxed floors are no more hazardous than shag carpets.

I never was much of a Boy Scout because the mention of hikes brought on a nervous sweat. Unlike most kids, I preferred the uphill part because it was slow and I could use my hands for balance, but when I reached the top, I would become hysterical because I had no idea if, how, or when I would reach the bottom. Usually I careened into a tree or rolled into a creek. Now I often wonder where I'd still be tumbling if some kindly scrub pine had not ended my descent for me.

I am no longer embarrassed about all of this among friends. They either don't come near me, or they wear shin guards and helmets in the event they must get near enough to risk my crashing into them as I get up from a chair or walk across the room. Around strangers, however, I still feel terrific anxiety every time my handicap shows up.

In college I lived on the third floor of the dorm, and after falling down the stairs several times, I understood why people at the bottom would holler up, "Is Hudnall on the steps anywhere?" before they would even start their climb. When my child fell off our deck straight to the ground, I rushed down the steps to help her; my injuries turned out to be worse than hers. Once when I mounted the three small steps leading to the podium from which I was to address the whole student body where I was teaching, I stumbled into a rail and spent the next fifteen minutes dabbing blood from my lip while trying to be a dynamic speaker.

There are advantages to my tragic flaw. My mother would never let me run errands. My wife insisted that I shouldn't walk the baby to quiet him down. People prefer to mix their own drinks at my house so that I won't have to pass them. And it's far safer to have someone else push my lawn mower for me.

I have adjusted well over the years and consider myself most fortunate to have kept a good job, made fine friends, and established an otherwise normal and desirable lifestyle. I even thought I had the perfect marriage and the world's most loving and understanding wife—until yesterday when she said, "Why don't you take up jogging?"

Footnote: See "On Being a Klutz"

Remember the Name Mercy Fair

When Mercy Fair returned a prospect card to our Admissions Office, several people commented on her lovely name. In a day and age when every third inquirer is a Jennifer or a Michelle or a Tiffany or a Brittany, it was refreshing to see a not-so-common name... and it was pretty.

A few weeks later, I made contact with Mercy in Augusta to tell her I would be visiting her school and hoped to meet her then. On the appointed date, Mercy and I arrived at the school Guidance Office at the same time, and the coincidence of our timing seemed to lessen any strain that may have existed when a fifty-six-year-old robust Caucasian male met a seventeen-year-old somewhat fragile African-American female—he being educated, well-traveled, and probably a bit imposing because of the nature of his "business," and she being a high school senior beginning to explore options to broaden her world.

I am an easy person to talk to, I am told, and yet I felt a bit uneasy for no explainable reason—at least, not right away. But as we began to talk, I came to sense in Mercy Fair qualities rarely seen in seventeen-year-olds. It was a combination of vocabulary, poise, and ingenuousness. When she said, "I've loved your college from the moment I saw the viewbook," I asked what in particular had appealed to her. She replied, "The pictures conveyed more than a beautiful place; they made me feel there were beautiful people there, too... the kind of people I want to get to know. I feel it is a place that would welcome me and allow me to become the person I know I can be." I could only offer weak-sounding assurances that she had captured the essence of our college, but I found myself saying to myself, "If any of this is true, please let it be so for Mercy."

She had mentioned that she lived with her grandmother, that her father was in some distant state and that her mother wasn't deeply involved in her planning. This had come about when she said without a hint of self-pity, "I am responsible for my future, both financially and in terms of what I do with my talents, and so it is important that I choose a college that will back me but not baby me."

It was a good twenty minutes into our meeting when Mercy asked about housing, and I used that opportunity to explain the value to be gained from living in a residential college community, everything from late-night conversation about boys to supporting one another during exams. Mercy let me finish my spiel, and then she said, "I have a six-year-old son, and it probably wouldn't be a good idea for him to live in a dorm. Could I live in an apartment nearby?" As I tried to answer cogently and helpfully, I couldn't dismiss the realization that she had had this child when she was eleven or twelve and that she had reached this point in her education very obviously in the face of obstacles most girls only read about. I am absolutely certain I didn't wince or gulp when she told me (in fact, I privately commended myself on a "business as usual" air); yet, Mercy was quick to say, "I hope this won't be a problem for being admitted. If it is, I've looked into other alternatives for my son, and I feel that they would be fine." I suggested we think about that later (and I *was* uneasy), to which she replied, "While I would like to have my son with me, a short-term separation while I get an education to better his life as well as mine would be all right." And then with a perkiness that gave one more dimension to this already-impressive young woman, she said, "Maybe I'll go into education; the vacations are great."

Just as I was about to wrap up this meeting and treat myself to some quiet time to reflect on how Mercy Fair had made my day, perhaps even my week, she said, "Mr. Hudnall, I am determined not to be another statistic, another unmarried, uneducated, black mother on welfare. Anything your college can do to give me the opportunity I need to get on with my life will be appreciated so much."

Never have I wanted more to have limitless funds, to be in a position to underwrite the cost of something someone wants badly, because never have I sensed such worthiness. Having anything at all to do with the future of Mercy Fair would be an investment in not just her future, but in the betterment of whatever world she becomes a part of.

Favorite Responses From My Reasonably Intelligent Children

As the offering was being collected at church one Sunday, my son leaned over and whispered that he'd like to have a quarter to put in the plate. As I dug into my picket, I took advantage of the opportunity to give him a mini lecture on what the real spirit of giving was all about. As succinctly as I could, I explained it was a more meaningful gift if the person actually earned the money he was giving away, and I ended my private sermon with the admonition that this was the last time I would fund his church giving. As I handed him the quarter, he whispered back, "Thanks, Dad, I understand. But you've got to remember that I'm still making up for that time I put a five dollar bill in the collection plate by mistake."

Daughter Elizabeth has always been spirited, a trait I applaud except when her spirit manifests itself in day-long tirades. When she was about six, there was one occasion in particular when her whining, fussing, sassiness, recalcitrance, and bullheadedness had been excessive. Realizing that my in-kind responses were getting us nowhere and thinking an early coronary might result if I didn't get some hold on the situation, I lowered my voice and said in the most imploring tone I could muster up, "Elizabeth, sweetheart, please understand that Mom and I aren't trying to upset you. We just need to make some decisions in your behalf, and all we ask is that you be pleasant about them." With her fists clenched at the ends of arms rigidly held at her sides, and with a red face and veins showing in her little neck, she screamed, "I *am* being pleasant!" Footnote: That same willful child is now an uncommonly strong young woman whose strength of character is enhanced by a gentleness of spirit that makes her a pleasure and, yes, often pleasant!

Elizabeth was a theatre major in college, and while children of friends with similar bents were paying to get much-needed experience in their field, Elizabeth landed a paying job, complete with housing, in a well-regarded repertory theatre for the first summer after declaring her major. Our pride and pleasure were magnified each time we heard our friends complain about subsidizing their children's employment. Except for an occasional five or ten dollar bill enclosed in a letter, we had no financial outlay. Our contentment soon gave way to deep depression, though, when Elizabeth called on the last day of the summer job to say that she had been "startled" to hear from her bank that she was $450 overdrawn. Exercising all the restraint I could muster up, I asked how such a thing could have happened. "Didn't you balance your checkbook as you wrote checks?" I asked. "Well, no," she replied, "because I could keep track in my head." Suggesting that that had seemingly not been a fail-proof plan, I then asked if she had ignored the bank statements. Her reply then was, "No, because I never got any; they are sent to me at school." With mounting frustration, I asked why common sense hadn't prevailed to put some skids on her spending, knowing the limited funds she was working with. To that she replied, "Dad, I feel bad enough that I have let you down this way, but for you to say I have no common sense really hurts. So I guess I'll have to prove to you that I do have common sense by telling you how this happened. I put a dent in the car and didn't want you to have to pay the bill, so I wrote a check for it myself." A sense of relief did not come over me.

One summer my son developed a back problem which worsened to the point of impending surgery. My disappointment that his condition precluded a summer job clearly outweighed his, but the relative seriousness of the problem was certainly my over-riding concern. Every time I saw this inherently lazy kid lolling around the house, watching TV and talking on the phone, I reminded myself that the curtailment of most of his activity really had created a bummer summer for him and that I shouldn't compound his situation by preaching. My wife went into full gear as the doting mother, fixing gourmet meals he didn't touch and testing her creative nature by devising all sorts of diversions. It was clear to me that my role was to make his unhappy circumstances as tolerable as possible, and this included not mentioning his hair, which got longer and longer because sitting in a barber's chair "would probably hurt too much." So, when the surgery was successfully behind us, I began to plan for his recuperation on my terms, beginning with a haircut at the earliest possible moment. Even as he was still foggy from the anesthetic, I held his hand and said in virtually one breath, "You're going to be fine and we are so grateful and I want you to get a haircut." His slurred reply was, "I'm sorry the surgery was a success."

"In general, the Muses
were the goddesses of fine arts.
In today's society, they'd probably be
the goddesses of show business."
Asimov, *op cit.*

*(Isn't it ludicrous to think of
Jennifer Lopez and Madonna as Muses…
or goddesses of anything lovely?)*

A peace-generating *Sparrows Club* gift just for you!

"A mighty Praise to God for YOU, Sparrows Friend!"

ROBERT SCHULLER

For all 2004 Sparrows Club members, Dr. Schuller has created, JUST FOR YOU, this beautiful gift…

Its peaceful, gentle sound will bring quietness to your home and spirit.

Fountain measures 8" high and 6" across.

Two beautiful, happy little sparrows sitting on a flowery branch with gently flowing water below them.

Etched deeply into the fountain's bowl are the encouraging words:

"His eye is on the sparrow, and I know God cares for me."

The detail is extraordinary.

The feathers almost feel soft…

The eye glistens…like it's wet and alive!

In many places around the 40-acre grounds of the Crystal Cathedral, one can find the peaceful, gentle sound of flowing water...

"World-class architects over my whole lifetime have impressed on me the importance and the calming influence of gently flowing water." —Robert Schuller

Gently flowing water in the Crystal Cathedral gardens, and in your home.

The majestic "Fountains of the Twelve Apostles" on the Crystal Cathedral grounds.

To make your Sparrow Promise for 2004, and to receive your beautiful, peace-generating fountain:

- Write Dr. Schuller—use the enclosed request slip and envelope.
- Call 1-800-9-POWER-9 TOLL FREE
- GO ONLINE at hourofpower.org/sparrows

"I am praying that YOU will be one of my 2004 Sparrows Club Friends…
…We cannot do it without you!"

The Glue

It doesn't embarrass me one bit to admit that the real strength in our family comes from my wife Martha Jane; if nothing else, being able to say this "in print" satisfies some of my need to be sure the world knows I know this. To most, I would seem to be the "personality" in the family. I'm more people-oriented and like action. Even though MJ has had her share of "prominence"—presidencies of virtually everything she joins, for example—she's often guilty of not asserting herself. There are those who would say that it hasn't seemed to hurt her in terms of affection and respect, but many people, especially those who first meet us, tend to gravitate to me and in turn perceive me to be the dominant partner. The very opposite is true... if "dominance" is measured in deep strength.

What are some examples of why I see MJ as the family's glue? One is that she never finds fault with any of us. Certainly, she corrects the children when they err, but there's no hint of character damnation. For me, there's never even the "correction." Somewhere in her system she has developed the grace to let other adults be who they are, irrespective of how displeasing a certain trait may be. She simply doesn't criticize anyone. Even more noble, she doesn't look for credit for anything. I remember once overhearing her conversation with a committee member for the Junior League, of which MJ was president at the time. From my end, I gathered that some new plan was brewing, and I heard MJ spew out one idea after another for effecting it. Weeks later, the League publication had an "applause note" for the other person and her "great ideas" for the such-and-such project. I made the mistake of expressing my indignation to MJ, whose response was, "For heaven's sake, Bert, what difference does it make whose idea it was as long as it worked?" I learned a little something then—about her and about life.

Perhaps the best explanation of why this woman deserves so much credit (to hell with what she thinks about that!) comes from the time when we were expecting our second child. Three weeks before the due date, we were dressing for a symphony performance when there was a sudden gushing sound, and I looked over and saw MJ standing in a pool of blood. She had hemorrhaged. I remember feeling a panic unlike anything I'd ever felt, but I also remember that MJ wasn't displaying the same anxiety. Instead, she said as if there were a master plan in place for such occasions: "Call the Taylors to look after Elizabeth while we go to the hospital. I'll call the hospital and tell them to alert Dr. Zammit. And, oh, please get a towel—a red towel—so I can clean some of this up." As I whirled around like a loose dervish, MJ calmly went about her self-assigned duties, including packing a little bag, as if she were getting ready for a weekend trip.

As we drove to the hospital, my heart racing faster than our car, I felt MJ's hand on mine on the steering wheel, and she said, "We both know this isn't normal. But we don't know that there's anything dreadfully wrong, and until we know that, worrying is a waste of energy. And if we find that there's something serious, even then we shouldn't worry because that'll sap the kind of strength we'll need." And then with a wry grin, she said, "And you're driving much too fast." *Footnote: the baby—our magnificent, now twenty-three-year-old son—was fine.*

Most mornings, Martha Jane spends fifteen or twenty minutes reading something uplifting. This private time grounds her for the day and gives her the peace to accept the day's happenings with grace. I should do the same, I know, but I get the same kind of spiritual sustenance from her.

A Vocabulary Lesson

Teaching "big words" to adolescent boys was probably the greatest challenge and also the greatest joy in my early teaching days in boys' schools. The groans I would get when I announced a vocabulary exercise were audible in the county, but I didn't relent, always pointing out that one day they would find it necessary to communicate in something other than slang and monosyllabic words. By the hardest, I persevered. Three incidents relating to all of this stand out.

One evening as I was finishing dinner in the boarding school where I was teaching, a colleague came up and said he felt he should renege on our plans to go to a movie because he had some papers to grade. After he left my table, Charlie, sitting next to me, asked what "renege" meant. Applauding his inquisitiveness, but knowing I shouldn't be too extravagant in answering, I said simply, "It means 'to back out of.'" And then I cautioned, "And remember, a word is no good unless you use it." Several months later, Charlie was again at my table following a holiday break, and I asked him how his had been. He replied, "Well, Mr. Hudnall, it really wasn't very good. I guess you know that teenage boys do drink beer, and I had some in my father's car one evening to take to a party. Just as I was reneging the car out of the driveway...."

I gave a class ten words to learn the definitions of, advising them that the shortest definition was usually the best. I also asked that they write each one in a sentence. The next day, Bill said to me as the class began, "You're a sly one, Mr. Hudnall." I had no idea what he meant, and he went on to say that I had tried to fool the class by giving them five words that meant the same thing. Knowing well that not even two of them had anything at all in common, I asked what on earth he was talking about. Bill's reply was, "Well, if we use the shortest definition like you told us to do, five of the words mean 'hence.'" The sentences he contrived accordingly were ludicrous.

The word 'oscillate' was one of the day's words, and after telling the class that it meant 'to swing backward and forward; to vibrate like a pendulum,' I decided to spice up the exercise by advising them not to confuse it with 'osculate,' meaning 'to kiss.' Of course, that only served to confuse one boy who, when asked to use the word in a sentence, said, "The girl in the swing was osculating so fast that she got dizzy and fell on top of all the boys who were waiting to pump her."

Calliope was the chief Muse,
and her name came from Greek words
meaning *beautiful voice.*

(Somewhere in the transition
between then and now we've lost something;
calliopes are used in merry-go-rounds.)

Amid Adversity

My father, a physician, died at age fifty-two when I was a senior in college. In November of that year, he began to talk irrationally, and tests revealed that he had an orange-sized brain tumor. Colleagues and family members who are physicians speculated that he must have known his own condition for some time, and given the unlikelihood of its being a benign tumor, he had shielded us from the suffering as long as he could.

The tumor was removed, but it was a virulent type which had clearly penetrated other tissue. For much of the next three months, he was mostly nonconversant. Occasionally, he would mutter something, usually about THE WAR. He had been in Europe during World War II, and it had had a tremendous effect on him, not for the good. My mother used to say he had come home a changed man—no less fine or loving, but clearly marked by what he had seen. Now, when he wasn't in control of much of anything, war-related comments were prevalent among the little bit he was willing to talk about.

From his dying, two memories remain especially vivid. One of them had to do with his preoccupation with war. I had come from college fifty miles away to spend the weekend with my mother, who had set up residence in a nearby hotel. I arrived at the hospital just as a nurse was about to give my dad a shot in his backside. She told me I was just in time to pull Dad toward me so that she could administer the shot, which I was happy to do. As I lowered him back, he looked up at the nurse and asked, "Were you in the War?" She replied in an understanding tone, "Well, no, Dr. Hudnall. Why do you ask?" Without missing a beat, my dad said, "Well, you should have been. You'd have made a great tailgunner."

The other memory was a more poignant one, truly something I am forever grateful I was there to see. During his last days, Dad was in a coma. My mother sat at the bedside except for occasional breaks, and nurses were faithful in the extreme in attending to his needs. In the final hours—and we had been told that's what they were—he developed a somewhat violent, seizure-like flailing of his right arm and hand, and nurses were virtually unable to restrain him satisfactorily. The condition had developed while my mother and I were out of the room, and when we returned we saw the staff about to strap his arm to the bed. My mother asked the men to let her speak to my dad. They stepped aside, but certainly they must have thought such a thing was futile. While his arm pounded on the bed, my mother took Dad's hand and whispered in his ear, and his body became relaxed. For the next couple of hours, she sat holding his hand and rubbing it, and there wasn't the slightest activity. He died that way.

I never questioned my parents' devotion to each other, but theirs wasn't a relationship characterized by open affection. Yet, at this last possible opportunity I learned something very important about relationships, about the depth of unspoken love. To this day, I can't hold my wife's hand that I don't realize that it gives me peace and that one day it could perhaps provide me the ultimate solace.

Starstruck? Not Me

Debbie Reynolds married a Roanoke man during the time we lived there, and I immediately began constructing a good reason to have her speak at our school. I didn't want it just to be for the glamour of saying "Debbie Reynolds is coming." Short of her singing and dancing, I knew nothing about her, certainly nothing about her brain and substance. So I bit the bullet and called her, expecting to go through several layers of secretaries and managers. To my great surprise, her husband answered the phone and offered no demurrer when I told him my reason for calling. It was the kind of "I'll get her" which you and I would say if someone had called our spouse. In a flash, Debbie was on the phone—perky, welcoming, and very receptive to my questions about if/how she might do something for our school (I didn't want to "line her up" until I heard what she had to say).

To my delight, she proposed addressing a small group ("where I can have good rapport") on the importance of self-discipline, of goal setting, of persistence. We agreed that our older middle schoolers might be the appropriate audience, and with no hesitation I suggested a couple of dates and she said, "You name it." How easy!

Sooner seemed better than later, and with the cooperation of the middle school teachers, we arranged a time and site for the next week. Debbie's presence wasn't to be an occasion for press coverage or a shot of glitz into the life of a normal school. It was to be an "educational experience." Obviously, there was some talk about it, but nothing sensationalized. Everyone was being perfectly rational and composed until I simply mentioned that I thought I should be the person to pick her up on the appointed day. That evoked some good-natured ribbing about the self-appointed perks of being the school head and about being starstruck. I didn't read anything else into it and said it was far easier to take that kind of heat than the kind that would come from choosing someone else.

The appointed day came, and off I drove to pick up Debbie Reynolds. I was conscious—perhaps too conscious—of just how unsensationally I was treating this. I even said to myself, Starstruck? Not me... ha, ha, ha.

When I arrived at the house, her husband met me and asked me to join him in the den while we waited for Debbie to get ready. I prayed that didn't mean the star's primping for a bunch of thirteen-year-olds would make us late. If ever there were idle conversation, it was then. The house was certainly pretty. Roanoke is certainly a friendly town, our school is certainly well-regarded, "Mrs. Reynolds" is certainly kind to do this, ("Please call her 'Debbie'"), and, to myself, I certainly hope she comes down those stairs soon.

Then I heard footsteps coming down the narrow, spiraled staircase at the end of the den, and I suddenly realized I must be sure my voice was deep enough and my manner cool enough as I rose to greet her. Thinking that a wrap-up comment to the husband before greeting Debbie was both polite and a clear indication that I wouldn't fall all over myself to greet the star, I looked him squarely in the eye and thanked him for his cordial reception and good conversation, and then I turned to her. With outstretched hand to meet hers, I walked toward her and said with a broad smile, "Hi, Bert, I'm Debbie." It was all downhill from then on.

Where There's Smoke....

Both of my parents smoked, and I hated it. Both children smoke, and I wish to hell they didn't. My wife was a smoker when we met, and that was the only deterrent to my full-blown appreciation of her. Most of my good friends either smoke or used to. I have never smoked, but I am considering starting. I think it would represent strong character. Let me explain.

No one can say smoking is good or good for you. While I still raise a skeptical eyebrow on the second-hand smoke issue, I have to say there isn't much that's defensible about smoking. HOWEVER, I think the do-good, self-righteous, anti-smoking crusaders are often just plain unattractive people in their behavior, and I don't want to be associated with them. Their protests are venomous and they lose sight of the issue, seeming to damn the person, not the deed. A pillar of our church was so rude, so un-Christian, in her response to a smoker during the after-church social hour that I began to wonder from whence cometh her faith and spirituality. If it were always displayed in such hurtful ways, I'm not so sure we're from the same pew.

On the other side of the issue, those who continue to smoke, whether by choice or because they just can't quit, seem to be increasingly endowed with steely constitutions to combat the ubiquitous attacks on their stinking habit or, sadly, on them, themselves. Not to be able to smoke in a restaurant or an airport or any other public place sends the signal that their habit is distasteful to many people. But to be depicted as societal lepers, scorned and verbally abused, is quite unnecessary and, in my opinion, says far worse things about the assailants than the smokers.

If each of us assumed this same kind of stance in objecting to things or even to people themselves we didn't like, we'd have a pretty miserable society, miserable generally and individually.

I just don't want to be allied with people who attack behavior as if it were character-related. Actually, it says volumes about their own character. While I really don't think I'll start smoking, I will champion those who do smoke in permitted places as ones who are exercising a right amid the slings and arrows of cause-inspired critics who have lost sight of the fact that their own behavior is far more reprehensible.

Three other muses were:
Melpomene — tragedy
Thalia — comedy
Urania — astronomy

Those Rich Doctors' Kids!

In my small town, being a doctor's child gave me a reputation for being a "rich kid." Admittedly, we lived nicely, but we weren't as wealthy as some of the lawyers' families or the executives at the paper mill or rayon plant. And we certainly didn't match the wherewithal of the retired founders of the paper mill—good family friends who actually owned a mountain overlooking the town. Yet, in the big picture, we were on the "high side." But that needs some clarification.

I said "small town." By extension, my dad was a small town doc. He was up at 5:30, at the hospital by 6:30 for his rounds, at his office by 9, home maybe by 6:30, but often not to eat, just to breathe a little while, and then back to the hospital or to make house calls. If he was home by 10, he and we were lucky. If all things came together to justify having the evening meal with us, it was a treat we all cherished. It was during those times that I remember some of his remarks which make me wish over and over that he had had more time with us and that he had not died so young. One of them was the time he looked at me during dinner and said, "Son, it really bothers me that I can't be here more often with you. Just seeing you tonight here at the table makes me aware of something I hadn't noticed before. You have a lot of manners.......but they're all bad." Once he said to my brother, "George, I took up for you today when one of my patients said something about you." George, not knowing whether to ask or to be glad he had been defended, finally said, "What do you mean?" To which my father replied, "Well, Mr. Puckett said he didn't think you were fit to eat with the pigs, but I told him in no uncertain terms that I knew you were!" These weren't insults; they were words of love uttered by a man who wanted as badly to have more time with us as we wanted that very thing.

I have been accused of being a big stoic. Actually, I'm not at all, but when it comes to being effusive about upcoming events such as vacations, special programs, etc., I am a bit stoical because our family regularly had to change or even cancel plans at the last minute because of my dad's medical practice. He categorically wouldn't leave town when a patient was critically ill. Once, we nixed a vacation the night before the scheduled departure because someone had taken a turn for the worse. Another time, we had just gotten to the beach when a couple coming to join us reported the heart attack of a family friend. My dad returned home without flinching.

One really vivid memory is of the time he had consolidated all he had to do into the daytime hours of a Saturday so he could go with us to the West Virginia State Fair twenty miles away. Our joy was palpable. But halfway over the mountain, we came upon a recent accident with several severely injured people. We stopped, of course, and three hours later we were headed back home, having each done a little bit for the injured and the traffic snarl—but no fair.

Yes, we had some money by comparison, but we didn't have the time or full impact of love Dad could have given had he not been so dedicated. And even having the money wasn't a compensation, because my brothers and I simply weren't indulged. A dime might have been all we got when we needed money for a coke. "They only cost a nickel, don't they?" My first car was my dad's which came to me when he died—not the way I'd have preferred to get it.

When Dad died at age fifty-two, my mother dutifully tried to get her "affairs in order." This meant getting an auditor to write to all of those patients who, according to Dad's records, owed him thousands of dollars. Predictably, most of those people replied with something like, "but Dr. Hudnall said we didn't have to pay because we can't."

We were actually pretty deprived in a larger sense, because we just didn't have the benefit of this magnificent man's full influence. The little bit we got, however, represented another kind of wealth, one that more than offsets anything else.

Sunday School: A Life-Threatening Experience

Going to Sunday School was every bit a part of my childhood routine as going to school. And I liked it. As a Baptist, I knew more about the Bible than most of my friends, and I looked forward to Sunday mornings because I found the lessons and socializing to be really enjoyable. Until one Sunday when I was five, a day that was a real turning point in my life.

As the teacher was helping me put on my coat at the end of the Sunday School time, she said in a sickeningly sweet and soft voice, "And next Sunday, Bert, you will be promoted." My heart stopped. Puhmoted! It sounded for all the world like "beheaded" or "castrated." I was terrified, and worst of all, I was afraid to tell my parents for either of two reasons: they wouldn't believe me, or I would find that they were a part of this scheme. The following week was hell. Every thought related to how I could save myself come Sunday. The smile on my Sunday School teacher's face kept coming back to me, and I couldn't believe that such a demon lived in the body of that nice person.

When Sunday morning came, I had such a headache that normally I shouldn't have had to go on that account alone, but because I feigned headaches to get out of almost everything I didn't want to do, even a legitimate one got me nowhere. As my mother sent me off to Sunday School, I tried to be brave, but I started bawling as I walked down the sidewalk to church. We lived next door to the church, and so it was okay for me to take this last walk alone.

As I got to the church, an escape plan became apparent. A clump of bushes next to the steps leading up to the door into the Sunday School room seemed very protective, and after glancing around and seeing no one (because we lived next door, I was always late!), I darted into the bushes and crouched there for the duration of the Sunday School time. I heard the door open an hour or so later; then

I saw many sets of feet go by and heard many happy voices, causing me to wonder why I had been chosen to be puhmoted. Whatever the reason, I had now found how to protect myself from such an awful fate, and for several Sundays after that I took my refuge in those bushes. Each time, I would come home with a full account of what the Sunday School lesson had been about because, after all, I knew my Bible!

It was when my mother ran into one of the teachers downtown and was asked why I wasn't coming to Sunday School that I was found out, but only after my mother had protested vigorously that I had, indeed, been coming every Sunday. When Mama said she would take me personally the next Sunday, I felt some security because I had concluded she wasn't in on the plot since she hadn't seemed surprised I was still around after that first threat of puhmotion.

Sproull Dean

It was a jolt to hear my mother say she thought Sproull Dean was a father figure for me. My dad had died when I was twenty-one, well past the time when kids need fathers in the traditional sense. But many years later, I've come to realize what she meant: that adult influences similar to a father's are never unneeded. Many boys/young men have coaches as their mentors; other have artisans or a caring neighbor. Military men, ministers, and movie stars may all be direct or indirect influences on a young man's life. Mine came in the form of Sproull Dean.

And "form" is a key word. He was a rotund, cigar-smoking, ex-policeman who had been eased off the force because of a cancer that had claimed his vocal chords. With much practice, Sproull had learned to inhale and then burp out staccato-style sentence fragments in a gravelly voice. His vocal limitations also limited his job prospects, and I met him when he came to work as night watchman at Darlington School in Rome, Georgia, where I taught right after college. Sproull's duties were predictable. He monitored the school's front gate from 9 p.m. to midnight. Then he made rounds of our extensive campus to be sure doors and gates were appropriately locked.

Our friendship developed one night when he saw my lights on and rapped on my door at 2 a.m. He told me the students deserved a well-rested teacher and I ought to go to bed. Actually, what I remember most was since I was already up so late, I might as well raid the school kitchen with him, which might make me a little more pleasant the next A.M.! Such raids became an almost nightly ritual, and during those times I came to know a man of great substance, kindness, humor, and strength. I also got a preview of upcoming meals and often surprised colleagues with my random guesses as to the fare. Even better, I got advance notice on how Claudelle, the chief cook, would spell SHRIMP. On those rare occasions when we had that delicacy, Claudelle always posted a sign advising us of our limit—and not once did she spell the word correctly. It could be SHIRMP, SHRIP, SHIMP, SRIMP, or even SHRMIP. So, having seen the sign the night before, I'd amaze my friends with not only a menu prediction, but also the exact misspelling.

Of many Sproull Dean stories, the most memorable one relates to the time four of us teachers went to Atlanta for dates with Agnes Scott women. We went in two cars, both to accommodate dates more comfortably and to permit any of us to come home early or stay later, if either circumstance presented itself.

After a good evening, we all decided to come back at the same time, but the fellow I had ridden with had had too much to drink and so I drove. Halfway between Atlanta and Rome, my passenger got sick and I pulled over to let him do his thing. The other car stopped too, but I waved them on and said we'd be not far behind. Fifteen minutes or so later, we were on our way, and my friend mercifully fell asleep.

On the stretch of road between Cartersville and Rome—a four-lane road, but very quiet late at night—I decided to press the pedal to the metal to get home quicker. About three miles from Rome, my heart somersaulted when I saw the blue lights of a police car coming fast behind me. I was speeding and I had been drinking, and suddenly I envisioned a scandalous loss of job and all the accompanying ignominy. I practiced composure as I slowed down and pulled over, and then it dawned on me that if I could make contact with Sproull he'd prevail upon his former police colleagues to overlook this little indiscretion. Feeling somewhat more secure with this strategy, I rolled the window down and spoke pleasantly with the officer. He was not inclined to offer an in-kind response. Gruffly, he said, "Get out and put your hands on top of the car." I sensed my plan may not work, but I tried. "Sir," I said, "may I please take my friend back to his apartment?" I thought that would buy me time. The policeman observed accurately that my friend didn't seem too fazed by all of this—he was snoring!—and I should do as I was told. So, I got out, placed my hands on the car while being frisked, and then was asked to walk a straight line. I did so perfectly; and coupled with my non-slurred speech, I was certain

I'd be sent on my way with only a citation for speeding. Then came the question, "Have you been drinking?" Every single possible response flashed through my mind in a split second, and none seemed right. Clearly, a No would have compounded things, and a feeble "just a couple about six hours ago in Atlanta" would never fly. As I was trying to get the best combination of things articulated, he said, "Place your hands behind your back," and with that he snapped on a pair of jangling handcuffs. I was mortified. As he steered me toward his car, I resigned myself to a collapsed career in private schools and began deciding right then how to pick up the pieces, when, lo, what to my wondering eyes should appear?! Sproull Dean, wracked in silent convulsions in the back seat of the police car. When the first car had returned to school and reported to Sproull that we were on the way, he had radioed a police buddy to pick him up and lie in wait for this prank on his friend, Bert. Never mind that the school was left unattended, or the Rome police force was shy one man who should have been finding real criminals, or that, in fact, I was guilty of two pretty serious indiscretions which were laughed off. Sproull had had his fun, and I know it was inspired by affection.

From that moment on, I was immune to Rome law. I didn't purposely abuse the law or my exalted status, but I did find it amusing that police would wave to me as I zipped a little too fast through town or that I could return to a parking meter whose time had long ago run out and not find a ticket while those on either side had parking citations.

Sproull was a master mechanic, and so whenever I had a malfunction he would make the repairs—free, of course. One day, I asked him where I should take the car to have antifreeze put in. He blurted out, "You can do it. It's easy." Nothing about cars is easy for me, but he assured me he could tell me step by step what to do and this would become my breakthrough in mastering automobiles. He told me how much antifreeze to buy, how to drain what was in the radiator, and where to pour the antifreeze. On a Saturday morning, I took a deep breath and began. I did exactly as I was told, but when I had drained the last can of antifreeze I could see nothing in the radiator. So I called Sproull and accused him of telling me to buy too little antifreeze. He rattled, "No way." Then in what must have been a revelation that summarized the best and worst in me for him, he asked, "Did you put the plug back after draining the radiator?" Of course I hadn't. He hadn't told me to! And when I feebly tried to claim not remembering whether I had or not, he spoke his loudest sentence ever, "You're dumber than shit." The only good thing to come of that experience was I never again had to worry about doing anything mechanical.

Sproull stories are legion, but one more needs to be recorded before this becomes a mini-biography. After raiding the school's kitchen and checking all locks one night, Sproull decided we should go to downtown Rome at 2:30 a.m. and get a Krystalburger. Krystals are fast food stores all over Georgia, but the kind you drop in late at night and hobnob with all the night owls and reprobates in town. Each of us ordered two Krystalburgers—total sixty cents—and were relaxing when we heard something that sounded like gunshots and then screeching tires. Instinctively, Sproull got his sizable frame off the stool, put his hand on his sheathed gun, and darted for the door. In a moment of mindlessness, stupidity, or bravado (I prefer this one), I followed him. After he quickly ascertained there was no danger outside, he ran for his car, with me close on his heels. Just as I got to the car, I thought, He's going to say, "Get your butt back inside." But he didn't. Instead he said, "Hurry up." Off we screeched in the direction of the earlier screeching, all the while Sproull listening to static police messages which indicated a chase was actually in progress. When I realized that we were the car nearest the culprits, I had some misgivings about being there and knew I could do nothing about them. The long and short of this story is that "we" did apprehend the perpetrators, but I had absolutely no role to play, as I saw it. I shouldn't or couldn't hold a gun, I didn't think shrinking in the front seat lent any substance to Sproull's authority, and I wasn't sure how "Way to go!" or "Is there anything I can do?" would be appropriate. So, I stood around, looking and feeling totally useless and absurd.

As other police began to arrive, the "Hi, Berts" were slightly reassuring that I wasn't a total hindrance. And as the "real police" drove away with the thugs their former colleague had pursued and caught, Sproull said, "Thanks for your help." Such a simple little comment comes close to telling why this man meant so much to me. But not as on-target as the one that followed. I said, "I realize this was a pretty dangerous thing for me, and I could have made it dangerous for you by getting in the way." Without a hesitation in thought—although it came out in several phrases—he said, "Nothing's ever going to happen to you when I'm around, and you're never in the way. Friends aren't ever in the way."

Sproull died the summer I was taking graduate courses in Colorado. I couldn't get to his funeral, even though his widow Mary said, "He'd want you here most of all, but he will certainly understand."

A father figure? To be sure! Loving, protective, accepting of foibles, and understanding. To have had two such people in my life is something I can only accept as rare good fortune.

Did you know that *music* meant
Art of the Muses?

A Barrette Saga

What parent hasn't gone limp when his little girl finally has enough hair to need a barrette to hold it in place? And then, please name one of those parents who hasn't spent at least a college education's worth on the blasted things!

Elizabeth was bald for about a year and a half. When the first fine strands of hair appeared, we started Scotch taping bow ribbons on her head in order to give her an identifiable sex. When she started ripping them off routinely, we toyed with using thumbtacks—but we held off until that glorious day when she would become a miniature Breck Girl.

The first barrettes we bought came twelve to a package for nineteen cents. Within two days Elizabeth had lost or destroyed or flushed all but the purple one. She especially enjoyed wearing that one with her maroon and powder blue outfits.

The next package had two per color, and so my wife decided to part Elizabeth's hair—such as it was—in the middle and to use a barrette on each side. Of course, Elizabeth promptly lost one from each pair, while insisting—upon threat of a prize-winning tantrum—that she wear two at a time. So, as the supply dwindled, it was not uncommon to deposit Elizabeth at Sunday School with a red barrette on one side and a lime green one on the other. Never did the two barrettes go together, and seldom did either of them even remotely tie in with her clothes.

We began to sense a real problem. My wife's idea was that a larger, classier barrette might be just the thing, so she cut Elizabeth's hair to accommodate a single barrette. She bought a very special barrette, one that had a pop-art bird (it might have been a chicken) painted on it. The only problem was that Elizabeth's hair had been cut with the part on the "wrong" side, and the bird was always upside down. I always felt there was something sordid about having a dead bird on our child's barrette. Our efforts to return the barrette met with a "can't do—sanitary reasons" response from the store clerk, and besides, Elizabeth had become so fond of it that she wouldn't even let us wash her hair. Little did the store clerk know how right she was!

I finally resorted to stealing the barrette off her head one night and tried to explain to her that the Good Fairy had taken it to give to a little girl somewhere who didn't have a pretty barrette. After making it clear that she didn't think it was a very "good" fairy who would steal, she suggested that maybe we ought to replace it since now she didn't have one either.

My wife decided on one whose design had no right side up—a porcelain-looking metal barrette with a sweet rose painted in the middle. It smacked of being exactly right. The only problem was that it had two very sharp prongs, which my wife managed to dig into Elizabeth's head the first time she used it. We might as well have tried to get Elizabeth to swallow milk of magnesia as to get her ever to agree to wear the rose barrette.

Deciding that I really couldn't afford to feed my family and to keep Elizabeth's hair out of her face, I suggested two alternatives: either use whatever we had handy, or cut all her hair off. We first tried a tortoiseshell favorite of my wife. It disappeared somewhere between the bedroom and the bathroom five minutes after it had been placed on Elizabeth's head. Then Elizabeth's great-grandmother's silver, monogrammed, heirloom "hairclamp" broke on the first somersault. There suddenly were no more alternatives.

Who knows if she knew what we had in mind, but Elizabeth got to the scissors first and took care of the situation herself. I didn't complain.

Oh!

So just how much idle time do I have that allows me to analyze the vowels and reach conclusions about them? Whatever, I've done just that and drawn the following profound conclusions:

As our first letter, *A* signals so much that gets our lives started. Anything with an *A* gets read or done first, and it is the letter that tells us that what we've done has been done best. (It doesn't help to include a reference to Hester Prynne's Scarlet A, so I won't.)

E is said to be our most frequently used letter, and so obviously it's vital to communications. Just watching one round of "Wheel of Fortune" confirms *E*'s invaluable role in our lives.

For all of us with bloated egos, *I* is indispensable. Actually, it's a whole word and its absence would make many sentences nonsensical—just as its presence makes many sentences BORING.

Isn't it fascinating that we never adopted *U* as a word? How logical it seems that the opposite of *I* should be *U*, and not *you*—but then we'd get into the whole thing about subjective, objective, and possessive case. We're probably better off just leaving *U* to the Burmese for a proper name (U Nu, U Thant).

For all the importance of each of the vowels, I've come to think of *O* as the *best* vowel. Now, so that I can't be accused of being self-serving, I hasten to say that there's not a single *O* in any name in my immediate family. But just consider where we'd be without the *O*. It's in *love*, *hope*, and *joy*. It's twice in *good* and, appropriately, only one is needed for *God*. And consider this: if written well, it's the only vowel without a loose end; it symbolizes completeness (the proverbial full circle). It makes normal declarations all the more significant (O come, all ye faithful). It precedes exclamations of wonder (Oh, my!) or dismay (Oh, me!). It symbolizes desire (O, to be in England; O, for a thousand tongues to sing), and it gives oomph (notice the two *O*'s there) to fairly bland expressions (Oh, for heaven's sake). It is so important that adding it to the ends of certain words gives them a special something—

"right-o," e.g. Or how about "Right-o, buck-o." That *really* says it.

By itself, *O* can be quizzical as in "Oh?" or connote understanding as in "Oh."

Now that you've gotten to the end of this pithy piece, you're probably saying, "Bert, I think U are wack-O."

Museum comes from the Greek word *mousa* and meant Temple of the Muses.

(Can you imagine what they would have thought if they'd known about the Air and Space Museum?)

On Being a Klutz

Rome, Georgia, is a town whose aptly named Broad Street has two lanes of traffic in each direction, parking vertical to the curb, and a sizable island in the middle. Traversing it is its own hike.

One morning I took advantage of an hour between the classes I was teaching to run into town to get some provisions for a dance I was the sponsor for. First, I had to go to the bank to cash a check, and upon leaving the bank the "Don't Walk" light began to blink. As I anxiously waited for the cycle of traffic to pass so that I could get on with my mission in the limited time I had, a crowd of twelve to fifteen people assembled with me. When the "Walk" sign flashed we all struck out briskly for the other side, except that in my preoccupation with time strictures, I didn't take note of the slightly deeper drop between the curb and where I was stepping, and I simply fell into the street. Many in the cluster of people around me stopped to help me up and ask about my well-being. As I quickly picked myself up and brushed off my pants, I was equally quick to assure them I was fine, all the while gritting my teeth over my public awkwardness and trying to be pleasant as solicitous comments were made during our "crossing."

Perhaps because of the persistent distractions or maybe just because I simply wasn't being alert—the reason really doesn't matter—I reached the other curb and stumbled onto the sidewalk there, this time tearing holes in both knees. The same crowd of concerned new friends managed to become interested again in my welfare, but with a decidedly different tone. Such things as "Are you sure you are all right?" seemed to mean something more than a concern about my physical well-being. I made all the predictable protests about being too clumsy for my own good and even said something about being able to understand why this was happening if it were midnight after a fun party, but that probably simply fueled a few fires already lit in some of the minds of those people.

I quickly took haven in the five-and-dime store, my original destination anyway, and began to look for balloons and crepe paper. With time ticking away, I didn't give my mission much real care and was heading toward the checkout area when I became distracted by something on another counter—I can't even remember what it was. After pausing only long enough to satisfy my curiosity, I backed away, still looking at the counter, and suddenly realized that I was making contact with something or someone. Fearing it was either a display of something very breakable or a ninety-year-old who would also break if someone of my size fell on him, I tried to avert a fall by whirling my arms around, just like you've seen in slapstick movies. That only served to increase the momentum, and down I went, landing amid a bunch of boxes wrapped in plain brown paper, except for the one that I smashed sufficiently to show that I had destroyed a pyramid of Kotex boxes. And as I struggled to get upright as quickly as possible, but not quite quickly enough, I looked up and saw one of my street-crossing companions with an expression I read as "He's sad."

What's It Really Like?

The grass isn't always greener for me on the other side, but I am clearly guilty of having my head turned by the wonderful-sounding pace Mr. Jones claims for his life, or the feeling of being transported when I am in a particularly different and charming setting that contrasts with my daily place and existence. To my great credit, I've at long last come to a point where I don't covet something else, partly in acknowledgment that I'll never have it, and partly because somewhere deep down I know that nothing is as it seems.

One way I've coped with any craving to be someone else or somewhere else is to get right down to the basics. Friends or acquaintances who lead zippy lives have their own flip sides, and I simply need to know what they are. Almost always I find that my comparatively humdrum life has features those people covet, usually relating to simplicity. When I was a freshman at Washington & Lee, I had some wealthy, high-living friends from big cities. With my crewcut and protruding Adam's apple, I looked every bit of fifteen. These guys were always more robust and, most certainly, always more "experienced." I pined for their lifestyle with all its opulence. Yet, when any of them visited me in my hometown, they came away mesmerized by the fact that I knew everyone in town and was able to have really substantial conversations with a wide range of people. Probably even more notable was that our dog was known by name by most people. I overheard several of those guys telling their families about the weekend with Bert's family, and their accounts of what they saw and heard served to reinforce my own appreciation for what I had.

Yet, the lesson was always short-lived, because all it would take was someone's account of a holiday filled with uptown merrymaking, and I'd revert to my "wish I had that" mentality. And to this day, I still think that way on occasion.

I need to hear directly that the grass is actually dying on the other side, and so I have started probing to confirm that. Very recently, we were in Oxford, Mississippi, a town that charms the socks off me. Its Town Square, magnificent bookstore, consistently friendly people, appealing restaurants and bars where I could imagine myself a regular *a la* William Faulkner, whose home was in Oxford—all of that is enhanced by the University of Mississippi (Ole Miss), a small university which nourishes the town, and vice versa. We were there for less than forty-eight hours, installing our son in the University as a freshman and drooling the whole time that he would have this marvelous experience while we returned to boring normalcy. One of those evenings, we had dinner with new friends, old-time Oxfordians, whose frequent references to William Faulkner, poetry readings, literary conferences, even the Elvis Presley convention (he was born in Tupelo, only thirty-five miles away), made me agitate over how I don't have that kind of opportunity, I thought. So I asked, "Tell me straight. Would living here take the edge off my imagined bliss? As residents, do you love each day, or is there the proverbial other side?" To my great relief, the reply was to this effect: "Those things are our diversions. In daily living, we have the same political issues, the same traffic problems, the same taken-for-granted relationships, the same nuisances, the SAMENESS everyone feels about where he lives—that is, if he has to work for a living." And there I had it. Seeing and sensing new places as a visitor is enhanced because I am away from what is usual. My impressions are influenced by the unusual. I have the luxury to explore and absorb and, in turn, to yearn for more of it. But if I lived there, I simply couldn't enjoy it that way, and wanting to, the contrast would be even more of a jolt. I needed to hear that.

Geography

In a world made up of people with different cultures, different appearances, different religions, different philosophies, people who eat different foods, dress differently, and enjoy different entertainment, one very basic question comes to mind: on what—or whose—basis is something considered "different." By definition the word means apart from the norm. But who is the norm setter? Might it be sensible to try to steer our thinking toward understanding norms rather than calling it understood differences? The word connotes separatism, and while we certainly don't wish to be all alike, we may well find more harmony in seeing others as having norms we *should* understand than as having differences we *don't* understand.

I believe that teaching geography is a key to making this happen. I don't mean that knowing the difference between a tundra and a fjord will accomplish this, but it may trigger something that will help by seeing what makes Alaskans think differently from Norwegians. It may be that "teaching geography" isn't exactly the key, but rather impressing upon young people the importance of making the learning of geographically-related matters a kind of lifelong habit. Something as simple as getting out an atlas when you read about an event in Ghana or Bolivia or upstate Wisconsin so that you can pinpoint just where it happened will produce a mental image that will make the occurrence more vivid. The benefit of seeing other places' names and getting some sense of their proximity to anything else will be a bonus.

Then we must go an extra step in our minds and realize that other people have their norms and *we* represent differences, and, gee, I hope they're tolerant of them.

Political Correctness

Given today's perception of politics, isn't the term "political correctness" an oxymoron?

It would be laborious to cite numerous examples of politically correct terms and to dwell on and laugh at each one's foolishness. More than the phrases themselves, it's the mentality behind them that's foolish, and that's what I want to address. An example may be a good starting point.

As the director of admissions at a women's college, I came to be very sensitive to "how to say it right." That wasn't hard, for I had always thought girls, women, females, were superior to men in many, if not most, ways. Many high school counselors said I was more convincing than women admissions officers in telling high school girls the reasons they should consider single sex colleges, and on my own campus I was often applauded for my presentations. There shouldn't have been any question about my respect for and convictions regarding women.

Once, though, in a meeting, I referred to a group of students I had spoken to at a high school as "girls," a very innocent, offhanded allusion. I might as well have called them sluts or dimwits for the kind of reaction I got from one of those in attendance. "We are a women's college," she asserted with venom, "and it seems to me that our director of admissions should know that." I really didn't know where to start, or if to start, to defend myself. If she didn't have millions of examples of how and when I had done it "right," why should I get as lathered as she over something so stupid? But I did.

I began by explaining to her that I knew we were, indeed, a women's college in name, in makeup, and in what we produced (oops, that's probably reckless). HOWEVER, those sixteen and seventeen-year-old non-males whom I met in high schools were GIRLS. Ask their parents. Ask their teachers. Ask their friends. They had boyfriends and girlfriends. Their own perceptions of women were not themselves, but their mothers, aunts, etc. I could have gone on and on about why they were girls, but didn't.

Instead, I decided to explain how happy I was, for the college's sake, that it was I and not my colleague who was drumming up business for our institution and how, with her mentality, the enrollment picture was jeopardized because keeping students was as much a part of enrollment as getting them and it may serve our administration well to do an in-depth study of those who decided to leave before graduation to determine the correlation between the overall figures and the number of those who had been exposed to this particular colleague. I sounded very much like Julia Sugarbaker on "Designing Women" as I rolled on.

And all of this leads to the "point" of my diatribe. Of course, we should all be sensitive to others' feelings, and if saying something one way instead of another helps to preserve those feelings, then let's try. But mightn't we also make *having* feelings the real issue over those who make everything "politically correct?" Shouldn't they learn to do a little swaying with the punches when they are displeased? Is their determination to be correct more important than understanding innocent motives? If so, we've gotten to the root of things right away. Caring for others' feelings isn't more important than their own agendas after all, despite what they may say their motives are.

Getting to the crux of this whole thing, I have to say that needing to be politically correct is but another sign of a personality I simply don't like anyway. These people are usually too self-important to suit me. The mere idea that they are the arbiters of correctness is annoying because the things they pretend to be right about just aren't more important than most other things, including understanding, kindness, and selflessness. Oops, again; all three are traits I'm not showing here.

Death, I Know Where Your Sting Really *Is*

Burying my mother was about the hardest thing I've ever had to do. But I'm not speaking only about its emotional impact. Certainly, that was paramount; because my mother and I were very, very close, I felt her death deeply, even in the knowledge that it was timely. Her last five years had been inactive, bedridden ones, with diminishing interest in virtually anything except for family. This magnificently beautiful, vital (she was doing the Charleston at age seventy-two), generous woman had become the proverbial near-vegetable, and so her death needed to happen, albeit bringing with it a sense of loss never imagined.

But that really isn't what this musing is about. Rather, it's about the ordeal of burying her following her death. First, the young minister of her church declared that he would do a "regular" burial service, meaning a fill-in-the-blanks kind of eulogy and perfunctory remarks. That wasn't all right. My mother's grandfather had been the founding minister, there were windows and Sunday School classrooms named for the family, and before her illness my mother had been very active in church matters. More importantly, the church mattered to her very much, and she contributed even if she couldn't attend. In his four years at the church, the minister had not visited her even once, and so he couldn't be expected to feel fervently about her. But I did. And I was determined we would have a "proper burial." So, I gathered some close friends who were known to this young man, and together we got the point across that he could and should do a little homework and make the service fit the person.

Having accomplished that, I then set about to get flowers for the coffin. The family wanted red roses and iris—a seemingly simple enough preference. But she was being buried on Valentine's Day, and so roses were at a premium. That was a perspective held more firmly by the florist than by me, and he persisted in trying to dissuade me from buying roses. "Why not carnations?" he asked. "Two reasons," I said. "Mama hated carnations, and I hate carnations." Then he suggested how effective a few "well-placed" roses would look amid a "sea of iris." The image was appealing, but the idea of a compromise was not. When he finally said, "Bert, these roses are going to cost you a fortune," I said, "Look, Clarence, I'm only going to bury her once. How much will they be? Here's a check." He may have had to turn away some Valentine clients, but Mama's coffin looked beautiful.

A few weeks later, I began to look into a marker for the cemetery and was steered to the "best stonemason for miles around." I visited the plant, met with the manager, and explained my wishes, which included being sure the stone matched my father's which would be next to it. I was told they would travel the sixty miles to my hometown to look at Dad's stone, which I thought reflected good sense and the kind of attention I wanted for this pretty emotional project. A few days later I received a call which began, "Mr. Hudnall, we've been to the cemetery in Covington. Are you sure you want us to use a stone just like your father's? It's top of the line and very expensive. We have others that almost match it and are much less costly." Without flinching, I replied that I really didn't want something that "almost matches," and so I authorized them to order the similar stone. Not too long afterwards, I was called to come and see the rubbing of the epitaph which would be chiseled into the stone when it came. It was perfect, and so I gave permission to do the work and take the stone to be placed at a time when the weather was best for them.

They called when that had been done, and my wife and I made plans to drive to Covington the next Sunday afternoon to see the last "official act" related to Mama's death. Some emotion welled up as we neared the cemetery, as I would be seeing Mama's name on a tombstone—so final. That emotion was replaced, however, by puzzlement emanating from an instinctive reaction that something wasn't exactly right. And then it became apparent what was wrong. The epitaph was on a slant! I turned my head each way to see if that made any difference. I even tilted my body to see if maybe a different position would level things out. Then I tried closing one eye at a time, but each eye separately confirmed what both of them had seen. The damn thing wasn't even! I picked up a stick and measured the distance between the top of the stone and the letters on each end, and the difference was over an inch. My frustration was indescribable. I had paid for the top of the line stone, and for eternity anyone visiting would see a slanting epitaph. So, this moment of expected somberness became one of mild rage, and we drove back to Roanoke expressing our disappointment and incredulousness in every way possible.

The first thing I did on Monday was to call the plant and tell of my findings. Over every imaginable protest from the manager that I must be wrong, I assured him that a trip with a tape measure would prove me right, and that unless some force unknown to man had remedied the situation overnight, I would not be paying an additional dime and I expected the correction to be done. They had no choice but to acquiesce when the mistake was corroborated by their people, and so we started all over again.

Weeks later, I was told that the "rare stone" had come and the work had been done and I might want to look at it before they placed it in Covington. I quite agreed and drove to the plant feeling some slight relief that this little project was about to be completed. With two of the plant officials standing right beside me, I looked down at the new work and sputtered in disbelief, "You don't see anything wrong?" as I read my mother's name across the top of the stone: "ELIZABETH REVERCOMB HUDNALI." There hadn't been room for the leg of the last "L" and so it had just been dropped off the edge! The men's effusive apologies drowned out my own moans of bewilderment. I'm never comfortable showing anger, and even now I was able to contain myself and say in a quiet, firm way, "Let's try it again. And let's agree that there will not only be no new charge, there won't be any charge at all." I alluded to how this would make up for the "pain and suffering" their ineptness had caused, and I am sure they realized that this was a far better course of action for them than what I felt I might be entitled to.

So, several more weeks later, I was called and asked to approve this next rendition of Mama's gravestone, and sure enough it was perfect. I was more relieved than happy and asked that they make placing it at the Covington cemetery a top priority. Two days later I was told it had been done, and immediately, but conditioned to some apprehension, we drove over for the viewing. It looked fine!

And the stones almost match!

Three more muses were:
Polyhymnia — sacred song
Terpischore — dance
Clio — history

Are You There?

I'm not yet a curmudgeon, but there are some things that are fast getting me there—prematurely, I might add. I used to say that the only thing I couldn't tolerate was intolerance, but as I age I am expanding my list of displeasures and, in the process, becoming more intolerant myself. Perhaps it's a form of wisdom, born of years of observing human nature and wondering how it is that intelligent people don't learn from their mistakes. A friend says the more she sees of people, the better she likes dogs. I think I understand. At least dogs learn to respond.

Responses—or the lack of them—is high on my list of irritations. Recently, I wrote two unsolicited letters to college presidents who had spearheaded initiatives which I felt deserved acknowledgment from another educator. From one of them, I received a copy of the same publication I had applauded, but without comment, as if I had requested a brochure. From the other, I've heard nothing.

This isn't a unique thing. Regularly in my work with a teacher placement agency, I hear that inquiries and resumes receive not even a form letter response. This bamboozles me. If a person in a leadership and hiring position can't find the time or way to say, "Thanks for your letter, but...," then I think some serious assessment is in order from that person's superior. Just what else is going unacknowledged?

A more frequent irritation for me is caused by people who don't know how to talk on the phone. I go out of my gourd when my chipper "Hi, this is Bert Hudnall calling to speak to John Jones" meets with NOTHING. So I go on to say, "I was told by Mary Smith that Mr. Jones would be able to give me some information I need." NOTHING. It's at this point I usually ask, "Are you there?" The really inept receptionist answers with a simple (very!) "Yes." The slightly more skillful one will ask, "What's your name again?" Whatever the response or non-response may be, my predictable question is, "Is Mr. Jones available?" to which the first person will say, "Hold on," and the second will say, "I'll see." The first person comes back to ask, "What's your name?" and then, "No," and the second says, "He's in a meeting." I offer to call back, and the first person says, "OK," (if anything at all), and the second says, "All right." Where's the training?!!? If I had a range of choices from which to get the information I need, I'd clearly not use Mr. Jones simply because of his telephone service, and I wouldn't buy stock in his company. It's not going to be around long anyway if that receptionist stays there much longer.

Clio meant *to tell of*—
thus, she's the goddess of History.

What to Do?

Several years ago, an organization of which I am a member needed to find a suitable spot for a retreat to plan the year's activities. We wanted some place near enough and yet far enough away to *be* away. Some friends—not close, but accessible types—have a beautiful mountain home with a lovely, spacious guesthouse. I assumed a nothing-ventured, nothing-gained attitude and called to see if they'd be receptive to our using the guesthouse for the day. We are all business people, responsible, etc., and I was able to say that we would provide the food for our lunch, cups for our drinks, etc. In other words, all we wanted was the site. Without a demurrer, the lady of the house was fully agreeable to the idea and even insisted that we use the main house since she would be away all that day. With profuse thanks, I accepted her generosity and assured her of the whole group's gratitude. Twice again before we met I expressed our thanks. One of those times was when, at her request, I came to the house to get a lay of the land, to be shown where various things were that we might need, and to be offered full and free use of anything we needed. The graciousness was genuine and more than expected.

On the appointed day, the seven of us met at the home which I had opened up earlier. All were justifiably impressed by the beauty of the place and its perfection for our purposes. Even though we were often distracted by our surroundings, we had a very successful meeting and left in the late afternoon reinforced in many ways. As the point person, I stayed behind to close up. After a double check of all things, I was about to lock up when it occurred to me to leave a note saying again that we were most grateful. As I wrote the note, I thought it sounded way too incidental for the kind of generosity that had been accorded us, and so I decided not to leave it, knowing I'd call the next morning anyway and also knowing we would send a gift, which we had already discussed.

The next morning, I made a call to a cousin who has a home business selling beautiful pottery, and I ordered a specially hand-painted large planter with the name of the hostess's home and some pretty flowers and was told it would be ready in about a week. Then I took care of some personal things before calling the hostess, wanting to give her time to get into her day. But before I called, I received a call from a friend—also not close, but perhaps feeling closer to me than I to her (or maybe not)—saying rather enigmatically that she heard I had used her friend, Peg's, house for a meeting the day before. Acknowledging that she was right, I then quickly asked if there had been some problem. Her reply was, "Only that Peg wondered why you didn't thank her." I was stunned! Perhaps attributing to myself a quicker mind than I really have, I immediately saw all the ramifications: the shallow sound my planned call would be heard with, the apologetic slant with which the planter would be received, the ill manners I would never live down, the insincerity with which any future words of thanks would be heard. I could only assure the caller that we were, indeed, most appreciative, and I had already made plans to demonstrate that beyond my verbal thanks. Knowing that the die had been cast, I wasn't especially perceptive in knowing the lukewarm response to what I said was predictable and sensing that she felt she had done "all she could do."

Believing in hitting things squarely, I could not fail to tell the hostess when I called that I had already heard (hoping that said something) of her concern about my seeming lack of gratitude and assuring her of just the opposite which I hoped she had perceived prior to our meeting and which we had made plans to "prove" subsequently. Her response was formal.

So what's the moral? Is it as specific as "always leave a note"? Or is it more general like "don't second guess someone else's response"? Or is it "never ask big favors"? Perhaps it's even more specific, like "call at 7 a.m. so that no one else can call first." Or maybe it's, "when you know you're right, to hell with busybodies."

Tim, the MagnifiCAT

We all know people who dote on their pets as much as many of us do on our children. A major difference as I see it is that children are punished for intrusive behavior whereas pets are fawned over and coddled. It's surprising to me how many of the families I work with in my counseling have dogs who are given free rein to paw, yip, scratch, or sniff while I am trying to talk seriously about a serious subject. I had an aunt who wouldn't take a vacation because she didn't want her dog to have to endure a kennel. A friend has a cat she lets wander throughout her car, including all over herself, while she's driving because she can't bear to leave the animal at home alone. Where animals are concerned, some people abandon judgment. I am jaded on this subject and probably sound callused and unfeeling. I prefer to think that it's just a difference in priorities. However, if I need to redeem myself in the minds of love-blinded pet owners, let me say that I have my own "My Pet Is Best" story, and, as my wife is wont to caution me against, I think I am right. You'll think so, too—or else it's that poor judgment coming into play again.

Tim is our inordinately beautiful, inexpressibly intelligent, uniquely appealing cat. Regularly, avowed cat haters say, "I don't like cats, but Tim's different." He has always been a "people cat." Where there are people to schmooze, he'll do it. If my wife and I are raking leaves, Tim comes to rest in the middle of the pile. If he hears activity at the church across the street, he'll go—to Sunday School, to midweek meetings, and even to weddings. When we take our dog for a walk on a leash, Tim follows along. We aren't thrilled when he saunters into a cocktail party, but always he becomes the center of attention and we are urged to let him stay. A friend who is highly allergic to cats persists in accepting invitations to our house, and over our protests that Tim will be sequestered she asks to see him (of course, she's his favorite person!).

Tim is a long-haired white cat with a fluffy orange tail someone called a "Velcro tail"—just stuck on, it seems. He is undeniably a show-stopper, but the curious thing is that he knows it, too. He always manages to position himself just right: in front of the multi-colored flowers, on the black sofa, squarely in the middle of the top step, or in the doorway. Several times, I have heard tourists strolling on our street in this most beautiful of cities (Charleston, South Carolina) exclaim, "Get that picture!" They're not talking about a charming garden or some interesting architecture; they're talking about Tim, perched on a neighbor's pilaster or lying on his back on the sidewalk with all four legs straight up.

We have worried that someone would be so overcome by this cat that he would disappear, and that concern became a reality right before Christmas in 1995. Although he had always been in total control of when he'd grace the homefront after a day of preening and prowling, it was unlike him not to come home at all. And when he didn't appear the next morning, we knew there must be a problem. We put signs on telephone poles and bulletin boards, we placed an ad in the newspaper, we even made contact with a couple of ladies whose worlds revolve around what's going on in Catdom. There is, in fact, a very active cat lovers society here in Charleston, and before long the word had spread and we were inundated with solicitous calls. It was all very gratifying, but Tim was not forthcoming. It's safe to say we never gave up total hope, but optimism began to flag after a couple of weeks, and we resigned ourselves to hoping Tim was making some other family as happy as he had made us.

A whole year passed, and occasional possible "Tim sightings" were pursued, but to no avail. Then one December evening we attended a Christmas program at the Cathedral some distance from our house, and a mild debate arose over the best route home. I opted for a known street while my wife preferred a more remote and less-traveled one, mainly to see a new set of holiday lights. In a mild snit, I turned onto "her" street, and about halfway down it Tim crossed in front of our car. I screeched to a halt, lowered the window, and called his name (yes, he does come to his name). He swung his head around, straightened up, trotted to our car, and jumped right in. Amid some weeping, my wife (who doesn't like cats, or so she says) cradled him as we drove home. We put him down upon entering the house, and the first thing he did was to go to the kitchen and paw open the cabinet where we had kept his food. He had obviously been well cared for, and we vacillated between wanting to thank someone and worrying that an ownership debate could arise if we tried to find who his recent caretakers had been. So we opted for telling a local human interest columnist about our story, and she wrote it up in her Christmas Eve article. In it, she told about Tim, the MagnifiCat, a title he well deserves.

Very recently, our neighbor, who had brought Tim a welcome-home present at Christmas, told us that she had seen a gentleman petting Tim, and she began to tell him about Tim's odyssey. The gentleman interrupted and said, "Oh, I know Tim. He lived with us for a year. We're glad he's home."